The Experience of Cancer Caregiving

Inside the mind of unpaid caregivers

Matthew Mckenzie FRSA BEM

Contents

Introduction 4

Chapter 1: The experience of cancer caregiving 5
- Finding the reasons for the caring experience ... 5
- Defining unpaid care 8
- The importance of the caring experience 10
- Why do people provide care? 11
- Applying caring experiences into positive experiences. 15

Chapter 2: The battle begins 19
- The impact of caring 19
- The battle of communication and dialogue 23
- The difficult battle carers face 26

Chapter 3: Battling for you 31
- Having someone to talk to 32
- I am being involved as the carer 38
- Access to peer support groups 39
- Helping to shape services 40
- Telling my story and raising awareness 40
- Having time for myself 42

Chapter 4: Involvement through lived experience 44
- Sharing your story 44

- How should you act as an expert by experience? 46
- Co-production..47
- Holding to account 51
- Ways to hold to account...................................51
- Carer engagement meetings 51
- Reading reports and feeding back. 53
- Being a Critical friend 53
- Involvement through surveys..........................54
- Carer group engagement.................................55
- Write reviews of services 56
- Speaking at events...56
- Carer groups for professional engagement.....57

Chapter 5: Looking Back 59
- So what next?..61
- Turning reflection into meaning......................62
- So, how do you reflect on experiences?...........63
- Turning difficult experiences into something positive. 64

Hope is King By Nadia Taylor 67
Being there 72

Introduction

This is my 5th book focusing on the importance of caring for someone unpaid. Most if not all of my previous books delved into the experience of caring for someone living with mental ill health. This book is my first book on the experience of caring for someone with cancer.

This book is for the most part aimed at unpaid cancer caregivers, but the book is not restricted to unpaid carers. Anyone including health professionals should have an interest in this book.

The book explores some of the reasons why a person wants to care for someone living with cancer. The book "The Experience of Cancer Caregiving" also points out some of the challenges a carer will face. Some challenges are in plain sight, but there are many hidden and unforeseen difficulties. A lot of these difficult experiences are not the carer's fault and they will have to navigate the path of health and social for a better caring experience.

As with most of my books, I point out the importance of networking, involvement and engaging with health professionals. It is vital experience of care can be used for feedback and development of health and social care services.

Chapter 1: The experience of cancer caregiving

So, it has finally arrived; you are now in that role. You are caring for someone with Cancer, and you are doing as much as you can. It was unexpected; it always was unexpected from the start. You never knew this would happen and have not prepared for it. Yet here it is. You probably picked up this book because you have repeatedly heard the term 'carer'. You might have seen a care plan and noticed the word 'carer'. You feel this could be you, but you are not sure. You may be more clued up on the term carer from what you have seen or heard.

- Finding the reasons for the caring experience

You know you might have to do tasks for the person you care for. This, of course, depends on the stage of the cancer diagnosis. You probably already have been shopping because the person you care for is far too unwell to do so. You might also be cooking and cleaning. A lot of the above is providing unpaid care.

You also might be chasing medical notes from health professionals. Ensure medications are applied and check out for any severe side effects on the person you are caring for. It does not matter if the person you care for is a wife, husband, brother, sister, or even neighbour. If you are trying to do most of the support, this provides unpaid care.

You may be attending appointments with them, which is a good idea for the most part, as you need to be part of the care plan; being involved in care means you understand your role and can also ask questions about what you might need to do. This also helps if your role becomes demanding; you might need to reach out for help. Caring for someone quietly does not mean you have to cope quietly. This means you will have to remind others that you are there to support and care, and doing so is a form of unpaid care.

You might even be visiting your loved one in the hospital, sitting next to their bedside, talking to them, comforting them, and providing that emotional support. You are being there for them depending on how unwell that person might be. This, again, is providing unpaid care and helping to wash someone if they are having a bad day, helping to dress them, and even providing emotional support. There is a book from Macmillan Cancer Support on speaking to someone who has Cancer; these are not easy skills to learn;

otherwise, there would not be booklets on these very things, but in the end, this is providing unpaid care. We also have Carers UK and Carers Trust, which provide a wide range of leaflets, booklets, and online information regarding the caring role. Information will be essential for your role, especially if there are changes in circumstances regarding the cared for's health.

It might be a roller-coaster ride fraught with difficult decisions. One day, the person you are caring for seems to be in good spirits; there is hope and a new way of looking at things. They will fight this illness, and you feel good to be by their side, helping them to fight Cancer. The next time you feel pushed away, the 'cared for' might feel down and depressed, their energy low, and they might even lash out. Sometimes, they will not say anything, or you might say the wrong thing and all that hard work might go down the drain. All this support is providing unpaid care.

Taking time out to be with someone and hoping they will pull through is not all about that. It is about problem-solving and what could help. You are looking around for information, and your battle, even though different for the person fighting Cancer, is still a battle, or you feel it might be a battle. If the person is too tired to fight, you will have to do the fighting; you will have to find ways to motivate or hope someone can pull through. Make no mistake, all this is in unpaid care. It is not always about providing motivation. It is also listening skills. You might already be skilled in listening, but then again, there are many courses, workshops and booklets on the importance of listening. It might be a struggle, but who else is the cancer sufferer going to talk to? You were their close friend or relative before, so why should that change now? This could be a test of that relationship. Still, there is no time to dwell on what needs to be done; it is now about how this should be done. This, again, is unpaid care.

- Defining unpaid care

Unpaid care is providing all of the above and more. You might be receiving some form of benefits, but you will not be paid to care; the form of benefits is to help you get by. There are campaigns to increase benefits, but this book is not about that; this book is to delve into the experience of the unpaid carer, just as I had to provide unpaid care. To be honest, I am on the side where we should not be paid to care; it should be about care on its own merit, but I agree that carers should not suffer financially due to doing their duty or love to be there for someone struggling.

Unfortunately, the term 'carer' is a loose term, as many apply this to care workers or health professionals. Even those in the middle of providing unpaid care do not think of themselves as carers. I have encountered many at the carer stalls I hold in hospitals. The number of cancer caregivers I speak to often are unaware that they are the carer. I listen carefully as they describe the person they care for and leave little or nothing about the support they should be getting. Perhaps this is a natural stage in providing unpaid care. It may be about quietly getting on with it and doing that role.

Maybe you think this way?

We just want to get on and make sure the person we care for has a better quality of life and a better experience of things. Why should they go through this struggle alone? Then again, why should you struggle as well? This book hopes to turn things back to the person providing care. We carers have an identity; however small that identity is, it needs to be heard. We are not just a cog in the system to be told to get on with it. We also have hopes, dreams, and our own needs for wellbeing. So much depends upon us as cancer caregivers.

- The importance of the caring experience

As you can tell by the book title. The book focuses on experience; however, without experience then, it is hard to learn or derive meaning from the caring role. I hope to share my carer experience with whoever reads this book. Not all experiences will be the same, which is to be expected; it would not be fair to say all forms of unpaid care are the same. Still, sharing experiences of care can be a way to connect with others. Sharing experiences is a form of peer support. Carers learn from each other and learn ways how to cope. Some experiences lead to self-reflection, a way to also connect with yourself. With these experiences, you can form an idea of who you are.

These ideas and definitions of yourself will probably change over time. I guess it boils down to the challenges you face as a carer. I do expect some experiences to be painful. For some carers, it can be traumatic, especially if they lost a loved one to Cancer. Experience forms our ideas, and ideas can help develop meaningful experiences. We are always learning from experiences, even if we do not think so. As mentioned before, experiences will psychologically impact us. Experiences will impact our thoughts and emotions. What we have gone through as carers will provide that perspective in life.

As caregivers, we sometimes need those experiences to take on the challenges that come our way. For some caregivers, those challenges will come fast, but remember, we all try to learn from those experiences, however painful or joyful. This is because the caring role allows us to learn from what works and what fails.

- Why do people provide care?

So, you are now on the road to providing care. You might not have made much of a decision on why you need to provide care, or perhaps you have thought long and hard about caring for someone with Cancer. This section is a reminder of why people do provide care. The information provided will perhaps give you some insights, experience, and some relief that you are doing the right thing.

Not everyone cares for the same reasons; family structures, relationships, and circumstances differ. There are even different cancer types and how they affect the patient. So why do people decide to provide care?

For me, the first reason people get on with the role is to be there for someone. They do not see themselves as a carer and feel providing unpaid care is just an extension of their relationship with the person living with Cancer. It might be a snap judgment to carry out the duty once the diagnosis is confirmed, but the carer will just get on with it when it is confirmed.

For others, it might be a sense of duty. It might feel like an obligation or a series of tasks that you must carry out. This was one of the reasons why I provided care in the first place. I felt obligated to make things easier for the 'cared for'. They were struggling, and I had the means and resources to chase things up and make sure their mental well-being was in place. I feel a large number of people provide care for this reason. It is a sense of duty that compels a person to care. Of course, that does not always mean this reason allows the person to provide the best care. Still, they will ensure they are there to support them even if the challenges are complex.

There are those whose culture and beliefs allow them to get on with the role. Specific ethnic communities will just get on with the role because they are expected to care for someone. Some ethnic minority carers might not even have a definition of a carer, but they will carry out the role. These reasons can again be closely related to duty. Still, the difference could be that a large family might take turns doing chores or carrying out caring roles. This is not always the case with all large families, as there are situations where members of that group leave it to the sole carer to get on with the role.

The above example explains why some people must step in and provide unpaid care. This is down to a willingness to take ownership of the issue. Some do not wait around to provide care. They will step in with a 'hands-on' attitude and take ownership of the role. The carer will want to take the lead and be known as the involved carer. There can be problems with such reasons as some might find the carer too involved and wanting things their way rather than putting the patient first. It is essential that someone has a carer who takes ownership and will carry out the role.

Since this book is about the experience of care, the other reason why people provide unpaid care focuses on how experience is applied to someone's life. Caring for someone close can give life meaning. It is hard to know what meaning the experience of care can bring. To some, it is a sense of fulfilling some purpose; to others, it is about being there, even if the experience is painful. To others, there is no meaning. It is what is expected of them. The meaning of life is a whole different book and a big book at that, but this is one of the most important reasons to care.

It is not only what defines us but a way of giving back care. This role can only work if the carer is of a certain age. It is hard to give back if you are a young carer. If you are too elderly, it is not fair to expect you to provide care as a means of giving back. The tragedy is that there are elderly carers providing care for someone. Most of the time, a spouse provides that unpaid care, but those giving back would perhaps provide care to a parent. Caring is not always an automatic thing. We cannot expect everyone to care at the drop of a hat. It takes an adequate upbringing, a sense of duty, and, most importantly, a form of love to care. Not everyone has these traits, which are the negative aspects of expecting someone to care when they are not the caring type.

Giving back care cannot be easily applied to young carers because they fall into that role. The following reasons can be applied to young carers. This reason is personal growth and a sense of meaning in one's life. If you provide care for someone at a young age, your life development can grow as you are exposed to unique challenges. The effects are not always positive if the young carer is not supported in their role. If a young carer is not identified, then the challenges can be too much, which can cause mental health or physical health problems. Experience of care can be a stigmatising role with lots of trauma and triggers.

The last reason I can think of for someone to provide care is that you know the person is getting the best care. You would not let anyone in your home to care for someone. You would want to carry out the caring role yourself, but only until you need some form of respite. This is one of the main reasons carers think long and hard before they give up the caring role.

- Applying caring experiences into positive experiences.

The caring role can be unexpected, challenging and full of anxiety for the future. Caring in itself can be a fulfilling role of love and determination. Caring need not have to break us down, but we must admit that providing unpaid care can be difficult today. So, how can caring lead to something positive in our own role?

I cannot speak for other carers, but I only share my experience and hope it provides some ways we can relate. Without a doubt for me, I felt compassion was the motivation for me. To see a loved one struggling with their health, I felt how that suffering impacted me. I felt that I was also struggling, not in the same way my mother's health was struggling or supporting a friend through Cancer. It was something emotional. I wanted to lessen the suffering somehow because the more pain I saw the 'cared for' go through, the more it impacted me. With the experience of compassion, it had filtered down into my other carer activities. I wanted to make a difference in the community. It did not mean I felt compassion for the community; it was more that compassion built my character and made me stronger.

The other character trait I feel is helpful in the experience of care is the use of optimism. Without optimism, it would be challenging to continue unpaid care. With the first sign of a cancer diagnosis, it would be possible for people to walk away. We somehow have to be positive for the diagnosed and ourselves. Some carers are told of the devastating cancer news, and understandably, optimism has begun to run out, but this does not mean that the caring role has gone. Some carers switch from the role of care relief to providing a better quality of death. So that they can be optimistic that they will be there for that person and make sure they share the journey to the end. So, the person living with Cancer does not journey alone. The experience of optimism has helped other carers as they felt there would be a positive outcome. Those carers will continue to attend appointments, continue to talk to their loved ones, continue to do the chores and continue to hope and pray. Optimism can lead to positive, caring experiences, but it is understandable when optimism runs out.

It can be easy to fall to pieces when taking on a caring role regarding Cancer. Hearing that someone close to us has that diagnosis is terrible news. It can make sense that many people will fall into despair, but as with optimism, some carers will use courage to face the caring role head-on. It can take courage to keep caring and being brave for the 'cared for' not only on the ability to care but to challenge professional opinions or ask for better support and services. No one was trained to be a cancer carer; most cancer caregivers are thrown into the role. Developing experiences to build courage can lead to a positive outcome, but it will take effort and sometimes luck. Even if the caring role ends, there still needs to be courage to carry on as a former carer role.

It's not always about doing things; it is also about communication. This is one of the most essential tools a carer can use for experience. There are books on talking to someone with Cancer; these can come from MacMillan Cancer Support. Even Carers UK, a national charity fighting for carers, also has tips on communicating with 'loved ones'. It is not always about communicating on a sensitive subject to the person living with Cancer but also to health and social care professionals. It is essential that carers use as much experience as they can to develop communication skills. For those who struggle to communicate, this can lead to adverse outcomes and experiences.

The last carer character trait that I think is useful when experiencing providing care is confidence. This is the ability to believe in yourself. Especially when no one else has the answers, caring for someone can be a lonely and isolating role. There will not be many who will go out of their way to give you confidence; a lot of what you learn will be down to your experience. It is necessary to develop confidence from experience. Sometimes, overcoming difficult challenges can build confidence, especially if you survive the experiences. It is essential to be confident even if the person you support does not feel confident about the situation. If they can see that their cancer situation is not affecting you, then this could lead to them feeling more confident.

Chapter 2: The battle begins

So we meet again. I am so glad that you have made it to chapter two. I hope I am keeping your interest when I share my knowledge. I was helping to care for a dear old friend who had prostate cancer. Those who know me very well probably already know who I was helping to care for. I helped him with projects on writing books. When he passed away, he left something with me—the ability to express myself through books and tell my story. You will find that as a carer, the caring role will impact you. Throughout this chapter, I will discuss the importance of telling your story.

- The impact of caring

The impact of caring can be felt in many ways. Depending on the stage of Cancer, you might find yourself mentally and physically exhausted. This might be due to doing the chores or helping your 'loved one' move around. If doing the physical chores was not hard enough, then exhaustion from mental anxiety will most likely impact you. Carers worry about the future of the person they care for. Carers often worry about themselves, and this can lead to a cycle.

One of the most common situations a carer faces is isolation and loneliness. Caring for someone can be personal, closed off and away from others. The stigma of Cancer does not help because some carers or cancer sufferers do not often want to discuss the terrible illness. I have experienced this when I run carer stalls at hospital sites; some carers find their experience so difficult that they do not want to talk and will quickly take a booklet.

To counter such awful experiences, carers might want the chance to relate to another caregiver. Having that connection to those who have similar caring experiences can often help. I try and attend Carers UK "Attend a cuppa" groups when isolation was making me feel low, I even attended my local carer centre support groups. Carer support groups allow carers to feel better, reduce isolation, and give carers a chance to talk about their feelings. Some carer groups even allow tools where people can develop skills to work through difficult emotions.

In the end, I started my own group aimed at those caring for someone with Cancer; I learned as much as I could from connecting with others. The isolating impact of caring for someone can sometimes be so significant that you can risk illness yourself, so it is important to try to connect with others.

As you probably already guessed, this chapter is about battling for you. Make no mistake, once you end up in that caring role, you are not only battling for the person you are caring for. You will have to try to battle for yourself. This can be all too easy to forget when caring for someone because the caring role is almost about putting the 'cared for' first. If you are caring for someone with Cancer, then there is that anxiety to battle as hard as you can for that special person. It is all too obvious that you will forget yourself. The hidden rule is not to forget yourself, but understandably, this can all be too easy.

One of the most significant adverse impacts of a caring role is financial hardship, which is made altogether difficult due to the cost of living. Do not think being a working caregiver makes things easier, as you will probably have to take time off to provide care and support. Recently, Carers UK launched a brilliant campaign to support flexible working rights for unpaid carers. This goes a long way to support people suddenly hit by the shock of caring for Cancer. Still, we cannot ignore the challenging situation working carers face.

Caring for someone with Cancer can be costly due to travelling to appointments and missing work to provide care, especially if the person living with

Cancer is the earner. Macmillian Cancer Support, a national cancer awareness charity, has excellent information on understanding financial worries and dealing with the cost of living. One way to counter rising costs is through information. I urge cancer caregivers to check the Macmillan Cancer Support website by typing "Macmillan Cancer support" into the search engine.

Another thing that can cause a challenge is how Cancer affects relationships. Not just relationships between partners but also all types of relationships. These can include family members, the young caring for older adults, or older adults caring for another family member. Once someone discovers they have Cancer, then there is a risk that their relationship with others will dramatically change. It will be difficult for some people to face things bravely. Other people living with Cancer will lash out, and the carer might take the brunt of things. Sometimes, carers will not know what to say because they are worried they will say the wrong thing. This leads to the next section of this chapter, which can be a tremendous battle regarding communication and sustaining the relationship.

- The battle of communication and dialogue

When I was helping to support someone going through Cancer, there were days when things were very dark for them. One wrong word I knew would affect my friendship with them. There were many mistaken things said through frustrations and misunderstandings. It was not long before I felt that empathy could go a long way to reducing the wrong thing being said. Rather than saying, "I understand what you are going through", I soon noticed I could never understand what my friend was going through. Instead, I would respond during difficult conversations, "I am sure this is a difficult time for you". It felt the statement was not too judgemental, and there was a chance to help counter those dark days of anxiety and depression.

There will be times that you, as a carer, cannot possibly know what to say. No matter what you do or say, there might be a terrible reaction from someone you are caring for. It does not hurt to admit you do not know what to say. One of the best-known things a carer can do is listen. There will be periods of silence for the person you care for, but if you listen to them, even in the most challenging moments, there will be clues on what you could say. Perhaps being a cancer carer will be full of mistakes; no one is perfect, so it helps to forgive yourself when you say the wrong thing.

A good way of sustaining a relationship with someone living with Cancer would be reassurance. Just saying you will be there for them can go a long way. They need not respond, but it can make a difference deep inside. Asking questions on if they would like something done can help in the caring role. I know it takes a lot of energy to do things, but that is what the caring role is about—doing things for that special person in your life. Unfortunately, much communication between the carer and cared-for might go down to guesswork. It's about vocal communication, tone of communication, and body language. How fast a carer can learn all of these things depends on the support they can get. It helps to identify that someone is providing care and then refer them to means of support; it could be workshops, carer groups or 1 to 1 support. One of the most useful for carers is education, which would be leaflets distributed to carers. Still, there is no substitute for group or personal connections. To have someone listen to our fears and concerns can make a world of difference to a carer.

It can be understandable that someone who is caring can bottle up their feelings of anxiety, anger and depression. Some people ignore these emotions because they are too focused on providing for the patient. There will be those who are scared to admit that they need psychological help, especially if their loved one is in the late stages of Cancer. I am on the side where it is essential to admit that you need help. There will be times that we experience difficult negative emotions and then ignore them. Still, the challenge is to develop tools to cope with such emotions. What we do not want is a double tragedy where the patient is suffering and the carer. So, I often hint to carers of those with Cancer that there is no shame in asking for help.

For a carer to ask for help depends on their circumstances; not all carers are alike, and it might take time for someone to open up for support. All I can say is that it is ok to heal, but do not forget to ask for help when needed. It is important to battle for yourself as well. Asking for help can be a battle in itself. It is difficult to know where to turn to to ask for help, especially if you are new to the caring role. I often feel carer support centres are an excellent means of support. There is usually one local to your area, and it is worth registering as a carer at the support centre. Most carer support centres belong to a network from the national charity Carers Trust. It is worth checking out the Carers Trust website.

- **The difficult battle carers face**

Carers suffer from many stigmas, which means people can discriminate against or form negative opinions about the caring role. Some view the caring role as superficial and lazy, but most understand it is anything but simple. Cancer caregivers have to carry out many roles.

One of the battles depends on how tired the person living with Cancer is. This leads to the carer doing chores around the house; a fair number of times, it could be down to cooking for someone too tired or unwell to do it themselves. A carer might need to help the person they care for get to appointments; this could mean lots of driving around and chasing medical appointments. If the carer was working, they could not always take time off. This could mean they have a job at home as an informal carer, plus the work they must do to earn a living. Depending on the job and level of caregiving, it is no wonder some carers can end up exhausted. It is important to speak to your employer about flexible work hours if you are finding yourself having to care for someone with Cancer.

There will be carers who have to help with medication, especially if the cared-for has difficulty accessing medication. The carer would have to ensure the person they care for takes those medications. It has been reported to me that some carers find some people hesitant to take medication. It might mean the person felt they were a bother to the carer and refused help. There might be situations where the cared-for feels no hope and wants to give up. Most of the time, the patient would be too unwell to take medications themselves, so the carer would have to support someone who takes medication and record any side effects. One of the things about side effects is how this can also affect the carer. Some carers can develop mental health problems due to experiencing the declining health of a loved one. Not all cancer sufferers' health will decline as some cancers, "If detected early", can be beaten.

A greater battle is the level of stress, depression and anxiety a carer can go through as they share the journey when the health of a loved one can decline. At my carer stalls at some hospital cancer centres, I often hear carers report levels of anxiety when called in by the person they are supporting. This is due to a cancer screening. They report a roller-coaster ride of highs and lows due to fear of the future. Most do not pick up any information from the stall. Instead, they discuss their fears and the challenge of accessing carer support resources. This leads to a political problem: the levels of cuts local authorities have had to face. Many community centres have struggled to remain open, which can cause people living with Cancer and caregivers to lack access to support groups. Some areas have resources for a support network, while others services are struggling. Quite a few centres offer counselling, but the carer must find other support means if access to such support is limited.

As mentioned earlier in this chapter, a carer peer group is often helpful for cancer carers. The challenge is finding one running in the local area. I have had to run my group online to cover a wider area. A lot of cancer carer support groups can be run from a cancer centre, but it can be a challenge if the carer has to travel some distance. Most might want to try their local carer centre, but not all carer experiences are alike. A carer group aimed at those caring for someone with mental illness is not the same as a group aimed at those caring for someone with Cancer. So, it can be difficult for cancer caregivers to find a carer peer network. There are cancer carer forums online, which are an excellent source of information, networking and contacts. Unfortunately, online groups require digital literacy, and not everyone has such resources, especially older adult carers.

So here we have it. Not all cancer caregivers will face the same battles; some will have more extensive support networks to help provide care;

this could be other relatives, better cancer support services, or even the diagnosis of Cancer, which could be easier to deal with. Some carers might be at a disadvantage, thrown into a world of anxiety and worry because they are not sure what the future will hold. Many will be placed on the line as health and social care services try their best to cope. Those services will focus on the patient, but the carer must make themselves known. It is important that services include the carer to the point the patient has a better outcome, including the carer themselves.

We cannot have unpaid carers neglecting their own needs because, by default, they have to also focus on their loved ones as the patient battles Cancer; the carer battles for the patient but will have to fight for themselves as well. When fighting for someone else constantly, it can be all too easy to neglect our own physical and mental health. Those who provide care must allow themselves to be identified, be empowered to speak about their role, and not feel guilty of thinking of their own needs. Carers must be given skills to help them communicate with their loved ones. Cancer is such a terrible illness it can quickly destroy relationships. However, there will be many situations where Cancer has brought people together.

Carers should not have to battle to access support. They should have access to a carer's assessment to assess their needs, raise alerts of any challenges, or at least plan for the future. Being a carer should come with its own rewards, as you take the lead in supporting someone you love. However, with stigmas, misunderstandings, neglect, and reduced resources, carers will be expected to battle not only for the person they care for but also for themselves.

Chapter 3: Battling for you

You might think this book has become depressing now that we have identified some battles. You might feel I have pointed out all the problems without providing answers or solutions. This chapter looks to address the importance of battling for yourself. I think the title of this chapter is a great answer if you have found yourself providing care.

Some things mentioned in the previous chapter also hint at solutions. One of the most important battles is ensuring you are identified as caring for someone. There is no hard and fast rule for carer identification. Still, one of the best ways to be identified is to register as a carer at the GP surgery or local carer centre or even be a member of national charity Carers UK. You might be recognised in the hospital discharge or care plans. Still, a lot of things in any hospital plan will focus mostly on recommendations for the patient.

What you want is a care plan for you. Any battle you take on must come with some plans for success. Below is a list of valuable things I found helpful when fighting for my own needs as a carer.

1. Having someone to talk to.
2. Educating yourself about Cancer
3. Wellbeing support.
4. Being involved as the carer.
5. Access to peer support groups
6. Helping to shape services
7. Telling my story and raising awareness
8. Having time for myself
9. Understanding my own needs
10. Planning for the future.

There can be more added to the list, but off the top of my head, those are the main things I felt were common for most cancer carers. To be honest, many things on the list can be helpful for many other carers. I will go through the list in some detail and explain why they are so important.

- **Having someone to talk to.**

Cancer can be an isolating experience. Caring can be personal, closed off and lonely. You will undoubtedly feel anxious about the future, and a lot can depend on what the patient does to battle cancer. You might feel guilty, angry and cut off from people. You will probably focus a lot of your efforts on caring for someone, depending on the stage of the Cancer. Worst of all, you do not want to discuss your worries and fears with the person suffering from Cancer.

You would feel that you are burdening them with your problems when the sufferer has enough to deal with already. This can cause cancer caregivers to feel guilty. Sometimes, the battles and challenges the carer faces must be discussed. So it helps to have someone to talk to. It could be other family members, a close friend or even a health professional. Cancer caregivers need to be very careful about who they talk to. If you talk to someone who is not sympathetic or understanding of Cancer, they can cause significant trauma or damage.

It is so essential you have someone to talk to who understands your situation. A good connection would be to other cancer carers, or if that is difficult, then you might have luck with other unpaid carers. Take note that not all carers are alike. Some carers experience easier caring roles, while other caring roles are a nightmare. Remember, there are online cancer carer forums that you can access, and some cancer centres run local support groups. Some cancer centres even provide 1 to 1 psychological support, but those will only be accessible for a few weeks.

To reduce isolation and loneliness, find someone who can listen. However, be aware that they might not always be on hand, and note that they cannot solve your problems. Respect your friend's time if you talk to a close friend, and you may find your support circle will grow.

- **Educating yourself about Cancer**

There are many different types of cancers. We have Breast, lung and bronchus, prostate, and colorectal cancers, and those are just the start. When I was first told that my old friend had a prostate, I felt guilty; I did not know what it was. I never expected to help provide support, but I spent a lot of time at his place, and it was not long before I had to provide care and support. Still, I did not know what I was dealing with and was scared the Cancer was deadly.

Stephen helped me support him by talking about Cancer, but I felt it was not enough, so I researched online. I made sure to look at the most recommended sites. So, the best websites are listed below.

Please note that website addresses change over time, so it might be best to google the website name.

A. NHS Website -
https://www.nhs.uk/conditions/cancer/

B. Macmillan Cancer Support -
https://www.macmillan.org.uk/

C. Cancer Care Map -
https://www.cancercaremap.org/

There are lots of other sites that can provide more information about Cancer. You even have booklets from Macmillan Cancer Support that are useful for finding more information about Cancer. You can order a copy from the Macmillan website, which I listed above. Other valuable information on cancers can be found on your local hospital website. These sites can be perfect for discovering the latest initiatives or treatments in dealing with specific types of Cancer. Cancer awareness events can also be a great source of information. Below is a list of cancer awareness events; you need not examine them all; just choose the one you are most likely caring for.

- Bowel Cancer Awareness Month
- Skin Cancer Awareness Month
- World Cancer day
- Breast Cancer Awareness Month
- Prostate Cancer Awareness Month
- Lung Cancer Awareness Month

There are many more awareness days, weeks, and months. I mentioned that cancer awareness campaigns are suitable for learning about Cancer because local and national events are running. You can attend conferences and seminars to learn about specific types of Cancer. You can even network and might meet other carers or patients. In the end, educating yourself about Cancer can often help reduce cancer stigma, and with that, many more people will likely live healthier lives and get tested or screened earlier.

- **Wellbeing support.**

This, without a doubt, is one of the most important for a carer. When I run my carer stalls at the hospitals, most carers stop to talk, not because they want to look for a leaflet, but because talking helps their well-being. Many carers are surprised such a stall exists and feel less isolated. Talking helps their well-being, but that is not the only thing. Looking after your well-being reduces the onset of mental health challenges. We focus on reducing anxiety, depression and mental negativity. Well-being support can be accessed from the GP if you mention to the doctor that you are a carer. It is essential you register as an unpaid carer at the doctor. Most doctors will notice that the carer will need access to support and should refer them to the local carer centre.

Talking about carer centres they are a great wealth of wellbeing support. Carer centres can provide the following.

- Information and advice
- Info on benefits
- Some might provide respite
- Access to support services
- Advocacy
- Emotional support
- Workshops and groups that focus on physical and mental well-being.

Carer centres can provide many more things, but the list above is a good example. You don't have to attend a carer centre constantly; you can look online for tips for well-being support. Again, only use recommended NHS sites or carer sites. Carers UK has excellent resources for carer well-being. I have put a link below, but if the link changes, you can google "Carers UK well-being."

    A. Carers UK - https://www.carersuk.org/help-and-advice/your-health-and-wellbeing/

Young carers can also check out other sites.

    A. Carers Trust - https://carers.org/about-caring/about-young-carers

B. The Children's Society - https://www.childrenssociety.org.uk/information/young-people/well-being

C. Young Minds - https://www.youngminds.org.uk/young-person/coping-with-life/young-carers/

There are many other sites, but Macmillan Cancer Support booklets are an excellent source of information on Cancer.

- **I am being involved as the carer.**

Being involved can mean several things. The primary use of being involved in care is being noted and identified by the health professional. Your views, opinions and concerns can be included in any health plan. If you are not involved as the carer, it can be challenging to take your views seriously. Remember, this chapter is about battling for you, so it is important to make yourself heard. In some situations, the health and social care professional might think again and include you to get your views. Make sure to let them know you support the person with Cancer. It also helps if the patient asks that you be included.

The other meaning of being involved as a carer could also mean getting your views heard regarding cancer service changes or service provisions. It is not right to always ask the patient how health services should be configured. Cancer impacts friends and families, and most carers who feed their views into changes regarding services will undoubtedly ask for their views to be heard and included. I will cover this more in chapter 4.

- **Access to peer support groups**

I have mentioned this a few times. It is so important carers have somewhere to be heard and feel they belong. Caring can be isolating and lonely. It is easy to make a mistake in the caring role, so to connect with other carers, we do not feel alone. You can find peer groups online or at carer centres; you might even find one running at the cancer centre. I will never forget a carer at my stall mentioning that there needs to be more carer peer groups because there is no one to talk to.

There are other benefits of carer peer groups, although not all carer peer groups are alike. Some groups allow members to slowly open up about their caring experience, especially if there is trauma in the caring role. Other carer peer groups allow carers to feed ideas off each other. When carers can express their ideas, they feel more confident and empowered. Some groups even allow carers to be part of the group even if the carer does not say anything. Each person will have a different viewpoint, and some will even raise concerns or ask for clarification on a challenge they are facing. Some groups are carer-led, and some are led by professionals, but at the end of the day, it is important carers have a chance to connect, share and learn.

- Helping to shape services

I will cover this in the end chapter, but briefly, it is linked to being involved as a carer. It means you are making sure health services include carers in their decisions. This is so important that I will dedicate a whole chapter to this section. Helping to shape services can lead to carer empowerment. As a carer activist, I have learned to promote carer inclusion regarding health services.

- Telling my story and raising awareness

This should not be a battle, but unfortunately, it can be for a number of cancer caregivers out there. The reason why is due to stigma and trauma. Depending on the experience of caring for Cancer, a carer will find it challenging to share their experiences. Sharing their experience or telling your story is important because many people, including other carers, can learn from that person's experience. Cancer is such a terrible illness that any lesson that can be learned could save a life.

The problem is how to tell a deeply traumatic story and where would you share your experiences? For me, sharing my experience of caring for someone started at carer support groups, but this soon progressed to conferences. I was scared to share my own caring situation, but at the end of sharing my story, I felt empowered because I felt heard. I felt for the first time that important people were listening to me, including other carers new to the role. In the end, I knew that I was raising awareness.

Of course, you do not have to stand in front of an audience to tell your story as a carer. You can write a blog post, a video post, or even a book. Just be mindful and confidential about what you say regarding the cared-for. People living with Cancer might still have their own stigma experiences, and they have a whole different story to tell.

Just remember that telling your story can empower you. It can make you feel stronger in your role and more confident about what you are doing and will become. With empowerment, you can set an example for others and feel that you are making a difference.

- **Having time for myself**

From the carer peer groups I run, I often hear this time and time again. A lot of carers just want time for themselves. There will be some carers who will spend so much time with the person they care for. The problem is the carer forgets that they should also spend time for themselves. It is not selfish to spend some occasion having some time for yourself. It is important you feel you can recharge your batteries. It is easy to fall into the role of being the patient's shadow, but this is unhelpful for the patient and the carer themselves.

What things can you do anyway? The first thing I suggest is getting enough sleep. Caring for someone can be tiring and demanding. So you must get enough rest. If rest is not what you need, think about what hobbies can give you peace of mind. The main reason for spending time for yourself is it can take your mind off things. To be constantly thinking about the caring role can drive you to distraction. It can also give you stress, which is something you should try to avoid. Unfortunately, saving time for yourself might not always be so easy due to the stage of the Cancer, but if you can find time for yourself, it is worth it.

Chapter 4: Involvement through lived experience

As tempting as it might be, you might want to avoid wanting to change the health system, especially if you have had bad experiences as a carer. I often say to carers that if you don't give feedback to health professionals about your experiences as a carer, then it would be difficult to cause change. Most health and social care professionals try very hard to accommodate carers. Still, there are far too few carer engagement leads to hear from carers like yourself. In the end, those caring for someone with Cancer will have to step up and be the voice to provide momentum for better healthcare.

- **Sharing your story**

It can begin with one simple step: sharing your story. Some stories of caring for someone can be so painful that it can be understandable why someone would want to forget about the experience. I think that is ok. We all need time to heal, especially if we are grieving.

On the other hand, sharing your story can be incredibly powerful. When you talk about your experience, it can offer waves of connection to others. It finally feels like you are being heard. You could tell your story to an audience at a conference or a carer's awareness event. You can even tell your story to help train nurses in the hospital. I only want carers to share their stories, even if the story is good or bad. We can all learn something from the carer.

When people get a chance to be involved in shaping the health system, it means they can feel valued. If no one listens to help celebrate your voice, then it can be easy to feel undervalued. Your experience can even help shape policies that include and identify unpaid carers. If you experienced the health & social care system while caring for someone with Cancer, then you would want to make sure such a system is improved to support unpaid carers.

Services should involve and include carers. This is because carers are the ones who also experience how the services have impacted the person they were caring for. Services should also be measured on carer engagement and identification. No carer should be left unseen and struggle to be heard. It might be difficult, but carers who want to help change NHS cancer care might have to break down barriers to be heard. If services involve the carer's voice, then there is no reason why involved carers cannot be ambassadors for NHS cancer care. If we all work together, then we achieve shared objectives. A service that includes the family and carers so they are not left in the dark when caring for someone with Cancer.

- How should you act as an expert by experience?

It might seem difficult to suddenly be told that you can automatically hold the health system accountable because you care for someone. What things should an expert by experience cancer caregiver look out for? Just to let you know, an expert by experience is a person who has experience of using services as either a patient or a carer. You might want to be involved in an NHS medical service as a carer.

If going for involvement, then some training is always helpful. This is especially important if you want to read procedures and policies aimed at providing better support to carers. As someone involved in shaping better NHS services, you will undoubtedly want to understand the Jargon. It is not always about reading; you will have to be fairly good at communicating your thoughts to professionals and even other service users. Sometimes experts, by experience, can see things health professionals cannot see. This is because unpaid cancer carers have used services, so they know what to expect. Health professionals might design services but might not always have experience using the system.

Remember that improving healthcare and carer identification requires teamwork. Carers should try to work with professionals as a team, and professionals should also try to reciprocate carer involvement at their local health NHS organisation.

- Co-production

Co-production is a way of working where service providers and carers work together to reach an outcome.

This can be challenging if you have not experienced much co-production. Sometimes, service providers are under pressure to produce a service, and things can become a tick-box exercise because the service providers have already made up their minds on the outcome. Co-production is a powerful tool, but only for those who have been through a co-production process.

This would mean getting some training as a carer or even a patient. There will be times when it is not possible to do everything, but they should appreciate your time.

However, it is difficult to work as a team if you are not informed about service provision and how it should include cancer caregivers. It might seem like a slow and daunting task for patient and carer experience leads to inform and help educate those who want to be involved and help service changes. Still, if the health service wants results, they must ensure carers understand the impact of health service delivery. The bar is still relatively high for unpaid carers to feel excited about becoming involved. Still, then this depends on the experience carers face when caring for someone with Cancer. The more significant the service's impact on the carer and the family, the more the carer would want feedback. However, carers must be informed on how to do this.

Carers who want to be involved must also be consulted and asked what would work when health services are about to be delivered. This could be through a simple survey or a workshop. If carers are not consulted about a service, it would be hard to know if cancer health services are making a difference, including families, friends and carers.

Once the consultation has ended, there is time for engagement, usually promoted via events. Some events can be held online or at a venue suitable for carer engagement. Of course, carers should also ask about engagement events, as waiting for consultation might never come, which could lead to second-guessing on the providers' part. We all want to avoid services that provide negative experiences, so it is important that carers keep an eye on engagement events or at least ask for them.

Cooperative work can be challenging to implement; it is about balancing professional knowledge and linking it to carers' experiences. We all want services that can be co-designed, but not all carers have the patience or talent to help co-design health provision. Sometimes, it takes a carer who is passionate about health and social care. Finding such carers to help co-design health service provision is like gold dust. This is more difficult when it comes to cancer carers because if the Cancer from their loved one goes into remission, then the carer is more than happy to forget about the experiences and get on with their daily life.

The last part of involvement comes from co-production. Co-production can mean many things, but at its core, it means people working together on an equal footing to develop service delivery. The problem is that co-production can mean difficult things to different people.

Co-production demands that everyone has something to contribute. We are building on people's experiences and hoping to make the services work for both cancer patients and carers. We need to value those who use cancer health services and would like them to return. Everyone has a capable answer and a work ethic. We understand carers' challenges, but we cannot be left in the dark about what unpaid carers require.

Everyone is capable and can make a difference; we just need to encourage and support our fellow carers to get involved. However, encouraging carer involvement is not enough because it can be a lonely experience. It is a challenging role since most carers only know what it's like to have an emotional connection with those they care for. To be suddenly placed on the other side of the fence to try and influence services can be a tightrope of what might work and what could go wrong. So, developing a peer-supporting environment is undoubtedly recommended.

A quick warning is that not all carers are interested in peer support; many unpaid carers are unaware of peer support. It must be vital that carers support each other as involvement should not be a competitive environment, even though, realistically, there are elements of who knows best. Many unpaid carers have gone through traumatic experiences, and the last thing they need is to be thrown into an environment where they feel isolated and cut off. Health professionals should represent a service that heals people; there is no excuse for involvement in an environment that becomes toxic to service users' health. Co-production is all about people and should end with empowered people to feel involved.

If co-production is done right, the end users and carers will feel confident about using those services because they feel they are part of the development services.

- **Holding to account**

If involvement is not your cup of tea, other ways exist to help influence services. It does depend on your knowledge about cancer services. Of course, the more care experience you have, the more knowledge you can propose about the impact of services. With this knowledge, you can query services and hold them accountable.

Health services must be answerable to someone and what better way for the services to answer to the end user. We must not forget that the carer is also the end user; whatever happens to the person living with cancer impacts the caregiver. There is always room for carer voices to be heard, especially if services are struggling. It can be very surprising regarding the knowledge families and cancer carers have about the impact of services.

- **Ways to hold to account**

Involvement in health systems and policies can be time-consuming, but there are ways to get your voice heard and change services.

- **Carer engagement meetings**

Every so often, the health services will run an event, which could be online via applications like Microsoft Teams or Zoom. Some events might be held onsite at a venue. If these events require carer feedback, then it is a must for you to attend. Such meetings usually focus on introducing new services or reconfiguring older health services. Still, it is important carers are asked for feedback. Some events might probably have workshops, seminars and panel interviews. NHS service providers might possibly update attendees on how their policies are working. Such engagement events can run from 2 hours to 7 hours. It depends on who is running the event and what they want out of it.

As a cancer carer, such events are a must, but finding them can be tricky. If you have internet access, then a website called Eventbrite can help you find such events. You might also be registered to receive news from your NHS hospital trust or carers centre. If you read any membership news, there should be updates on upcoming events. It is recommended that you attend local events because they provide the health services the cared for has used. Still, there are national events worth attending if you want to be updated—anything from NHS England, Macmillan Cancer Support or even Carers UK.

Sometimes, you might encounter lectures or webinars from university researchers. Still, the whole point is to give feedback, so attending NHS carer engagement events is a priority. Take note that carer engagement can mean two things. On one hand, it could mean involving the carer in someone's care. The other explanation is speaking to carers to allow them to share experiences and views.

- Reading reports and feeding back.

I am not the best at reading reports, although I often share news and updates with carers I am close with. Reading news about your NHS provider, e.g., hospital or GP surgery, can provide more knowledge you can hold accountable. It is advisable that you skim through any quality reports that hospital board members might produce. It isn't easy to hold to account if you do not know what the board members are responding to. One of the best ways to hold to account is to check if any reports include a focus on carers. Reports do not always have to come from NHS hospital services; you can view reports from health commissioners, Care Quality Commission reports or even news and updates from Carer charities like Carers UK or Carers Trust. Other charities like Macmillan Cancer Support are also a very good choice for reading reports, campaigns and updates.

- Being a Critical friend

It's not only about holding to account services; it depends on how it is done. There are many ways to do this, but I have focused on what a 'critical friend' can provide. A critical friend can be a carer concerned about the outcome of services. They want to know the implications and will ask difficult questions. The main thing is that the carer is expected to be part of the team regarding health and social care services. The carer should not shout, argue, or always find fault but should raise questions about the impact services will have on the carer and cared for.

As a carer, this is a role you might end up taking. There should be times when you praise a service that works well, but there also should be times when you want to question a service. It is always good to ask questions, especially if services impact your role as a carer. Do not be expected to know everything, but remember there are no silly or stupid questions to ask at an event.

- **Involvement through surveys**

Some hospitals and doctor surgeries allow feedback through surveys. They can be filled in on a note posted through a box, using an electronic device by pressing buttons to provide feedback. Most surveys can be emailed to the patient or carer, especially if you are registered as a carer through the NHS hospital trust or GP surgery. Surveys vary in length, but it is always worth filling those out even if you think you are not holding to account services. Just by responding to a survey can sometimes allow for anonymous feedback. The best thing about surveys is that you can take your time filling those in. When it comes to engagement events, you do not have time to think about things and must give feedback there and then.

The problem with carer engagement events is that you might not have all the correct information to give feedback. There are times when others in the audience give their views before you, and there will be some carers who cannot give feedback at all. Surveys might be boring regarding engagement, but at least you do not have to travel anywhere, and it can all be done at the click of a button.

- Carer group engagement

Suppose you are lucky enough to have your own carer group. In that case, you can even request that a health provider attend such groups to give updates and presentations. I usually do this with the carer groups that I run.

Carer-led groups can be run at carer centres, hospitals, or even online. Most of the time, it is part of the health professionals' remit to speak to unpaid carers. The only problem is finding who should speak to the group, getting the time of the group and speaker, plus supervising such groups. You might even need to take notes and help supervise the meeting so others can hear their voices. Most organisations tend to be happy engaging with carer-led groups since it shows carers can take the initiative and organise carers to be interested in feedback. It can sometimes be difficult for health providers to request carers to engage at an event, and it might be due to when carers have the time, interest, or commitment to attend feedback events.

- **Write reviews of services**

Without a doubt, this is something you should already be doing as a carer. Organisations like the Care Quality Commission (CQC) or Healthwatch depend on feedback about services. The CQC regulates many health services, and organisations like your local Healthwatch inspect services and give feedback to commissioners on the public's behalf. Without feedback, it is hard to know if services are working as they should. Getting a meeting with CQC inspectors can be difficult, so feeding back online is always a good idea. It even helps to read reviews of health service providers since that can increase your knowledge. Take note that you can always give feedback anonymously.

Another way to provide feedback is through the hospital Patient Advice Liason service (PALS). The hospital reviews all responses and should use such feedback to measure services. If the carer asks for a query, PAL services can vary in response time, but most should respond to questions or feedback.

- **Speaking at events**

Speaking at events can be daunting, but believe it or not, this is a way to hold to account. How come, some might ask? It is simple because, depending on the event, you are telling your story regarding services. If the event is about NHS services to include carer stories, then attendees can learn from your lived experience. I am sure there must be some health professionals in the audience, and it might boil down to you training the professionals on how services affect your caring role.

Telling your story to a crowd or audience is not easy. There are several reasons why this can be difficult. When we tell a story about our caring role, we touch on sensitive and personal experiences; some stories can be distressing or traumatic. Speaking to an audience also requires some skill. You need to speak clearly, try to keep the audience interested and be prepared to answer questions. Most carers who get involved in shaping services at an organisation tend to be invited to tell their story. Such events could be at carer conferences, awareness days, learning workshops, or staff training. Telling your story can become easier over time and is a great way to get involved. Attending events, even if not telling your story, is a must because you can also network with attendees and learn more about health and social care services.

- **Carer groups for professional engagement.**

Have you heard of the saying, "Weakness brought together makes strong?" Well, this is the case for unpaid carers wanting to make a difference. I am not saying carers are weak by default. We all need some form of strength, or how on earth do we provide unpaid care in the first place?

Still, holding to account as an individual compared to a group of carers clearly shows some differences. If you want to see what your local hospital is doing for unpaid carers then it can be possible. Still, you are more likely to get engagement if you belong to a group of carers asking questions. NHS trusts and local authorities tend to engage more with a group rather than an individual. Sometimes, you can hold whole organisations to account, but you would need to build up a reputation or represent carers. Not everyone has the time to do this, so it helps to link up with other unpaid carers and invite health representatives to talk to your group.

In my years of experience running carer groups, even this cannot be easy. It is not 100% certain that a health professional will answer your group, but it does help. The big bonus of having a carer group is a safe environment; you can develop a peer support network and look out for each other. The bad news is doing this takes a lot of skill and patience. You have to find out what other group members want; not everyone wants the same thing, which can even destroy whole carer groups.

Chapter 5: Looking Back

I want you to congratulate yourself on reaching the final chapter of this book. It is not an easy read, and if you skipped a few chapters, it does not matter; at least you are reading one of them.

I purposely placed this chapter last because it describes what happens when your caring role comes to an end or pauses for a while—all those who care for someone unpaid end up looking back. Many carers struggle with difficult experiences, and some experiences are traumatic. Some families and carers whose loved ones survived Cancer tend to look back while holding their breath, hoping the Cancer will not come back.

Looking back is an important lesson in the caregiving journey. In order to map our experiences, we have to examine the journey we took. Did we, as carers, make the right decisions? Were we distracted and took the wrong path? Maybe we took too long to do something, which caused a delay in support, or we just did not get enough support.

Different outcomes lead to different caring experiences, but looking back means we have a chance to learn from those experiences of providing unpaid care.

Suppose you have become a former carer due to someone reaching end of life. In that case, it can be an emotionally draining experience. I know that I have experienced this a few times.

Sometimes, our memories reflect on the day of a person's passing, or maybe we feel guilty because we are the ones who are left behind. We might feel that we should have done more. These feelings can be common, and I just want to mention that we should avoid feeling guilty.

We, as carers, have shared that special journey with our loved ones until the end. If we only reflect on and remember the difficult experiences, we miss so many things. Perhaps it is the small things we need to remember.

- The times we listened to our loved ones.
- The moments of joy, however small.
- Being there when things got tough.
- Even minor things like watching TV together.

The mind is an incredible thing. You really do not know what it can fully remember until you test it. If we let waves of emotions flood us, then we will forget the small moments. Sometimes, it is the small things that can lead to good experiences. Out of habit, significant and tragic events can creep up on us and cause painful memories to flood back.

This is when we need to remember to look after ourselves. Painful memories should be a sign that we need to find ways to cope. Some former carers decide to get out of isolation and go for a walk, even if it is to be among people. Some will phone someone close to chat about their feelings; it might be worth joining a group of former carers since you will all have something in common.

The thing is, if we do not recognise our vulnerability, then we risk poor health and well-being, which can lead to feelings of emptiness, depression and isolation. This might not always be the case, as some caring experiences are so tricky that the former carer might feel relief that the sufferer has passed on. Again, this might lead to guilt, but these feelings are natural. No one should want someone to suffer from the effects of Cancer, especially if they are trying to care for them.

The important thing is to be aware of your feelings and to make sure those emotions are not stopping you from enjoying things.

When we reflect on how we started our caring role, there is so much to learn. Life cannot always be lived forward; though time throws us forward, we need to look back. If we do not reflect, then how can we learn anything? This is one of the reasons I write books about the caring role; I want to share what I have learned from my caring role, which continues as I write this book.

- **So what next?**

So, you are looking back and reflecting on what you have been through. It might be good or bad, or perhaps you don't know. It is important that you are learning to understand it all. It might be hard to know what to do next. This is because the caring role can be challenging and demand a lot of attention. Still, it has all changed, and now you have to find ways to fit back into the community. People think the caring role is just that, a role to care and nothing else, but you have picked up many skills that are very useful to the community.

- As a carer, you would have to arrange appointments
- Communicate with others
- Plan for budgets on a shoestring
- Do household chores
- Learn new medical skills
- Be a good listener
- You might even have managed to become involved in services (see Chapter 4)

The list above only touches the surface, as there is so much more to caring than just waiting around. Caring is not a lazy role; it is an important life skill. Society or the community should not only encourage caring but also help to support it.

- **Turning reflection into meaning**

Besides learning from our experiences as carers, looking back at the caring journey and reflecting on things add meaning to our lives. Depending on the experiences, self-reflecting is a value in itself. We are what our experiences make of us, and we sometimes have to make sense of it all.

Sometimes, if the experiences are difficult, it does not hurt to get some form of counselling; there is no shame in asking for help. Still, things can trigger us to reflect back on memories; it could be a smell, a word someone has said, or even something you saw that causes memories to flood back. This becomes apparent, especially if you are a former carer to someone who passed away from Cancer.

Such experiences provide an increased sense of connection to the person you care for. No one else can experience how you feel about your journey as a carer. It is a deeply personal journey, and for most of the time, only you can make sense of it all.

- So, how do you reflect on experiences?

Thinking about a past memory is not enough. We have to try to learn from it, and if the experience was difficult, then perhaps we need to take what is positive from that past experience. Some people write their thoughts in a diary or journal to make sense of their former caring role. Some people write in order so they have something to treasure or that it is a way of getting things out of their system.

When writing about past experiences, former carers might try to describe an event that might have happened. If writing is not your thing, you can always examine how past experiences affected your feelings. What did you learn when you were providing a caring role? We all want to develop and grow but to do this; you need to understand where you came from. It is hard to forgive ourselves if past experiences show that we made many mistakes. Still, it is also so important that most of us are never taught how to provide unpaid care.

Providing unpaid caregiving is something that usually just happens. We, as carers, just fall into place and hope the person we care for does not succumb to a devastating illness. Unfortunately, Cancer can be a complex disease to recover from, and the impact can be felt across the family.

- **Turning difficult experiences into something positive.**

When reflecting, we tend to focus on major events, especially traumatic ones. Many carers note that their mental health suffers when their caring role has come to an end. This might be different if the person they cared for survived Cancer. However, those carers can continue to worry for the future.

If you have stepped into the former carer role, paying attention to the present might be necessary. We need to assess how we can turn the role into something positive and learn for the future. Some carers, through no fault of their own, become stuck and feel at a loss when their caring role has come to an end, especially if they have provided care for a long time. This is when we need to set goals for what the next journey will bring.

It is always worth it to speak to those who have had those experiences or search online for what to do when you have become a former carer. Suppose you are registered as a carer at the local carers centre. In that case, it is worth chatting with a carer support officer about your experiences. The centre might also provide skills and opportunities that can help your future role.

Of course, this is not always the case when trying to remove a negative experience from our lives. Those experiences help shape our direction and can give life meaning. Self-reflection can sometimes be uncomfortable, but it is necessary to look back because it can help us develop and grow.

Sometimes, suffering can lead to an improved sense of self-worth. As carers, we have come through a problematic caring experience. This could be for better or worse, but in the end, we have survived it. It is hard to say that no one learns anything from suffering. Still, we should conclude that pain certainly is a great teacher, not that anyone should rush to experience emotional or physical pain just because they want to learn something.

With self-worth, we feel that because we have been through those difficult caring experiences, we use the tools we picked up along the way and continue facing the future. These tools include strength of character, resourcefulness, being there for others, and even doing your duty or out of love. It is because we have been there for someone and shared their journey. These experiences can lead to a form of meaning in our lives as we try to be kind to ourselves and continue learning from others.

Hope is King By Nadia Taylor

Below is a carer statement from Nadia Taylor, who is provides her own experience on battling cancer for her loved ones.

No matter how challenging life is, it is precious and one never really reflects about it as much as when a cancer diagnosis or bereavement come and hits you like nothing else does. It is a cliché, I know, but when that dreaded piece of news comes, life changes at a drop of a hat. Fear floods in first, actually not fear but sheer terror: of the unknown, of losing all and everyone you hold dear, of how painful it might be, of how long you have to put your affairs in order, of when your final day will come…

One moment you are on your way to see the doctor, half expecting bad news due to the symptoms you had been experiencing, half in denial that nothing like that could possibly happen to you. Then suddenly, you feel like you are thrown into a vortex and violently spun when in reality you are actually stunned, unable to move or speak at first - a large mass lodged in your throat, mind crowded with questions - but lips uncooperative and unable to move to verbalise them. And then, immediately, the very human thought of "why me, how can that possibly be happening to me"? Chances are we may feel angry and we may even challenge God and ask: "how could He do this to me"?
The reality is that there is no rhyme or reason why these things happen. Why not me? Why should I be

immune from such a thing, or from anything at all really?

This dreadful illness in the myriads of forms it afflicts us and manifests itself can really bring out in each of us myriads of feelings, experiences, expectations but also ultimately, resolve and hope. It is so dependent on who we are as individuals, what our frame of mind is, what stage in life we are at and our own abilities to cope, or not cope. The latter of course can change depending on what life had thrown at us even prior to such dreaded news: some of us are incredibly strong and resilient no matter what. Such people can always, somehow, find a positive side to things even if it is to make a conscious decision not to crumble but to face what is coming with strength, positivity and resilience. Admirable qualities but I would be a hypocrite if I claimed to be one such individual. I am more like the others – frightened, panicking, sad, lost (at first at least!).

I believe we all have our vulnerabilities, whether we would admit to them or not. Feeling overwhelmed is perfectly natural, a normal human reaction to facing one's worst fears and one's mortality.

The news slowly processed - then comes living with cancer. Now the real challenge starts. Whether a patient or a carer, cancer really throws you into the fires of human suffering. Radiotherapy is meant to kill the cancer cells but it does not discriminate and damages the healthy ones too. It also makes your skin painfully sore, your mouth too, you feel sick, do not feel like eating at all, you lose your hair but you think to yourself: "ah well, hairdressers are expensive!"

If radiotherapy was not enough, chemotherapy follows soon after. Oh boy, you constantly feel nauseous and are actually sick all the time, completely exhausted, your hair is all gone, you have a funny taste in your mouth which is full of sores, your skin changes too and on a good day you think to yourself that your teenage acne was not that bad after all. You are dizzy, out of breath and your memory is like a sieve – a sieve with very large holes! Pardon the language but speaking of holes, you either have diarrhoea or could read "War and Peace" on the loo straining with constipation! You just can't win - constant infections, easy bruising, weight loss, nerve problems, urine, bladder and kidney problems... You name it, it comes your way!

Another side effect not many talk about is the loss of friends! Ah yes, the folks around you: all meaning well but at times you just want them all to go away and leave you in peace. Some understand that and keep a respectful distance, others, well, they just become distant. Maybe they do not know what to say or how to say it, maybe they just can't be bothered or maybe you do not want to bother with them. You are conscious of how little time you may have and all of a sudden you become excellent at managing your time.

You begin to evaluate what and who is important and despite the occasional bout of self-pity and, I am being honest, the ocean of tears, all of a sudden you start getting yourself organised. Slowly, Heaven only knows from where, but hope begins to surge within you; hope and strength because humans are fighters. You think to yourself: "Well, not me! I am not giving up, I am not giving in! I will fight! I am fighting, day and night and I will take my chances!

And this is what it is all about! Life is precious! Each and every one of us is precious, precious to ourselves, to our loved ones, to our friends and social circle, to everyone we have ever known, to all those who will come after us. Whether they judge us or learn from us, they know we leave a legacy and that legacy is part of our human experience.

Whether we win our battle with cancer and live on, or whether we lose, we are still winners. However short or long our lives are, we all leave a mark through simply having walked the Earth, having touched the lives of many others and having left our imprint in the library of human experience. Future generations will learn from us, from all our trials and tribulations so our experience will not have been in vain, our suffering is not in vain, our joy and achievements are not just ours but they are shared and will resonate long in the future through those we may leave behind as well as those who will come after us.

So, if you can, whether you live with cancer personally or look after someone who is fighting with cancer, however hard it is, try to remain positive and hopeful. However hard it is, AND HARD IT REALLY IS, keep fighting, do your best to enjoy every breath of air, every tough mouthful, every joke, every song and sound, every breeze, every drop of rain and every ray of sunshine because, long or short, life is precious, YOU ARE PRECIOUS AND HOPE IS KING.

Being there

Here I am
Being there
All I can do
Is say I care

Here I am
The best that can be
I am here for you
Just wait and see

Here I am
An unpaid carer
To be identified
We'll fight together

Here I am
I am never far
Through sun, rain and snow
I will be your guiding star

Here I am
I'll fight for you
Although I am not perfect
It's all I can do

Here I am
I said I will be here
I will take those blows

Because I care

Here I am
I will make that fuss
So you can get treatment
and other help we can discuss

Here I am
Trying to Be there
All I can do
I care for you

Poem by Matthew McKenzie FRSA BEM

Printed in Great Britain
by Amazon